NURSES

A First Look

PERCY LEED

GRL Consultant, Diane Craig, Certified Literacy Specialist

Lerner Publications ◆ Minneapolis

Educator Toolbox

Reading books is a great way for kids to express what they're interested in. Before reading this title, ask the reader these questions:

What do you think this book is about? Look at the cover for clues.

What do you already know about nurses?

What do you want to learn about nurses?

Let's Read Together

Encourage the reader to use the pictures to understand the text.

Point out when the reader successfully sounds out a word.

Praise the reader for recogni zing sight words such as *are* and *of*.

TABLE OF CONTENTS

Nurses

**Nurses help people
feel better.**

Nurses help people who
are sick or hurt.

They work with doctors.

Some nurses care
for new babies.
They help new
mothers too.

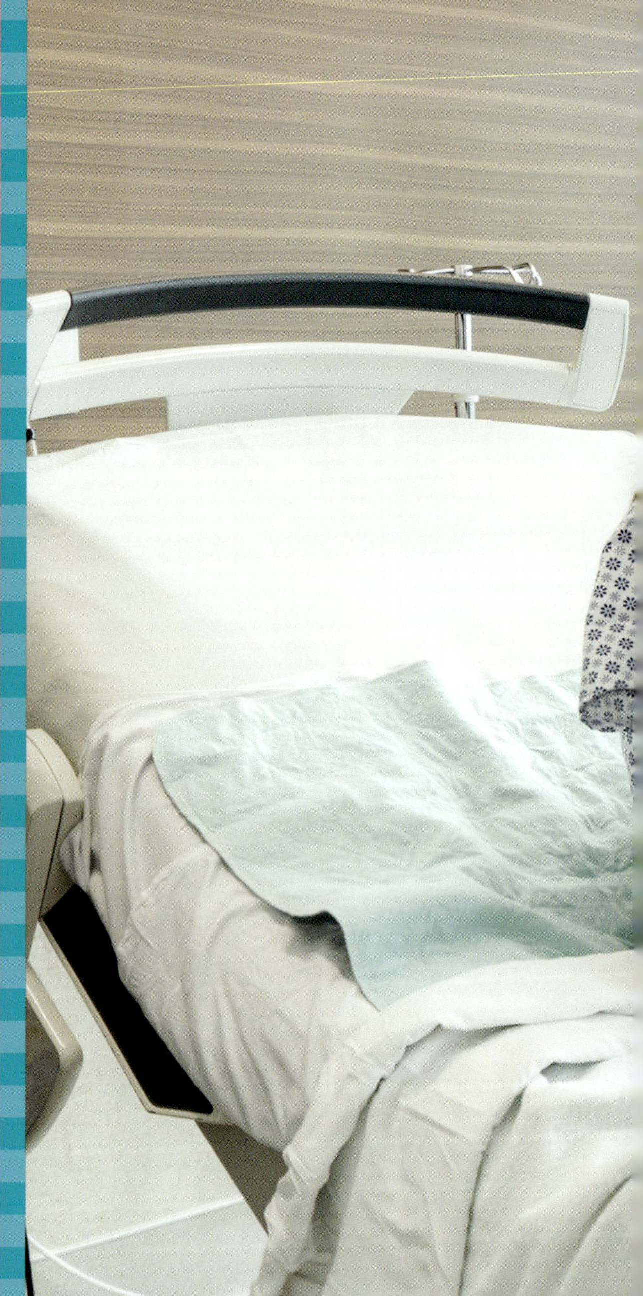

What other people
do nurses help?

10

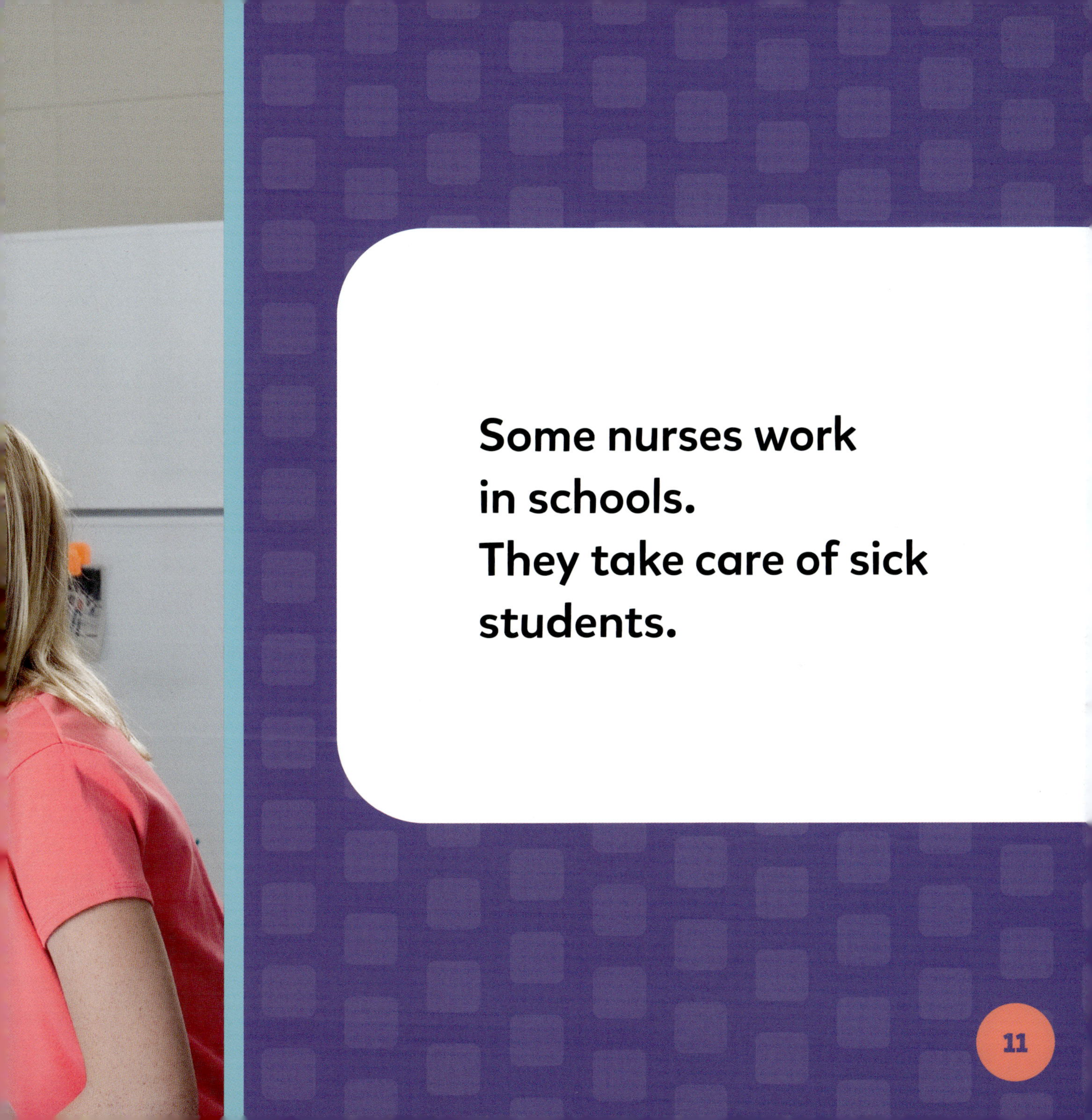

Some nurses work
in schools.
They take care of sick
students.

Nurses use tools.

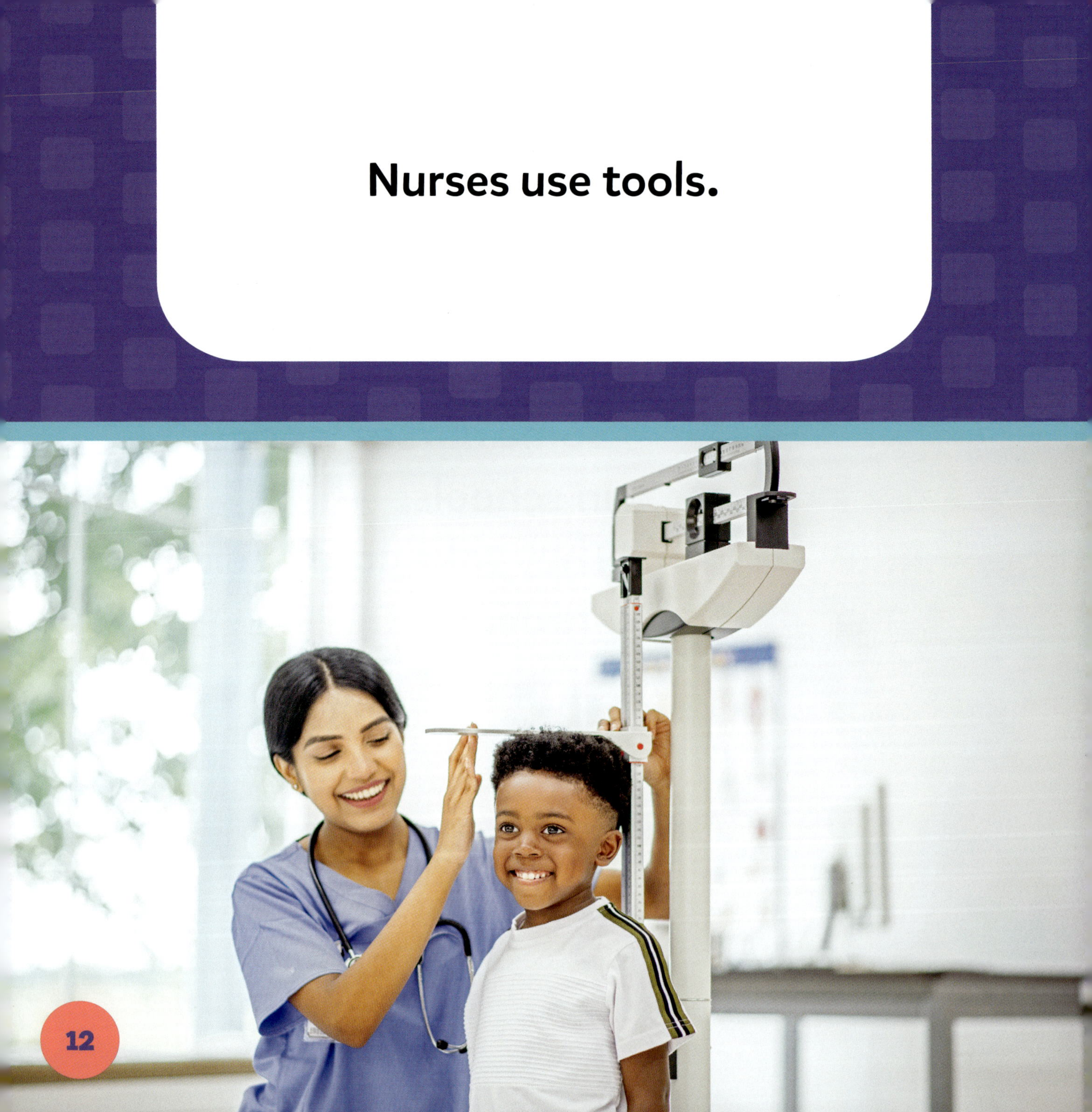

12

This tool tells nurses if someone has a fever.

13

Sometimes nurses
give people shots.

Nurses may wear
masks and gloves.
These keep them
safe.

How do masks and
gloves keep nurses safe?

Nurses go to school for many years.

Why must nurses
go to school?

19

Nurses work hard to take care
of people!

You Connect!

What is something you like about nurses?

How can a nurse help you?

Would you like to be a nurse when you grow up?

Social and Emotional Snapshot

Student voice is crucial to building reader confidence. Ask the reader:

What is your favorite part of this book?

What is something you learned from this book?

Did this book remind you of any community helpers you've met?

Photo Glossary

Learn More

Kaiser, Brianna. *All about Nurses*. Minneapolis: Lerner Publications, 2023.

Murray, Julie. *Nurses*. Minneapolis: Abdo Kids, 2021.

Waxman, Laura Hamilton. *Nurse Tools*. Minneapolis: Lerner Publications, 2020.

Index

Photo Acknowledgments

The images in this book are used with the permission of: © andresr/iStockphoto, pp. 4–5; © monkeybusinessimages/iStockphoto, p. 6; © LumiNola/iStockphoto, pp. 7, 23 (top left); © SDI Productions/iStockphoto, pp. 8–9, 13, 18–19, 23 (top right); © Brian Eichhorn/Shutterstock Images, pp. 10–11; © FatCamera/iStockphoto, pp. 12, 14–15, 23 (bottom right); © Prostock-studio/Shutterstock Images, pp. 16–17, 23 (bottom left); © Drazen Zigic/iStockphoto, p. 20.

Cover Photograph: © Halfpoint/Shutterstock Images

Design Elements: © Mighty Media, Inc.

Lerner Publications Company
An imprint of Lerner Publishing Group, Inc.
241 First Avenue North
Minneapolis, MN 55401 USA

For reading levels and more information, look up this title at www.lernerbooks.com.

Main body text set in Mikado a Medium.
Typeface provided by Hannes von Doehren.

Library of Congress Cataloging-in-Publication Data

Names: Leed, Percy, 1968–author. | Craig, Diane, consultant.
Title: Nurses : a first look / Percy Leed ; GRL consultant Diane Craig, Certified Literacy Specialist.
Description: Minneapolis : Lerner Publications, [2025] | Series: Read about community helpers | Includes bibliographical references and index. | Audience: Ages 5–8 | Audience: Grades K–1 | Summary: "Nurses help people who are sick or hurt get better. With accessible text and full-color photographs, young readers learn about the importance of nurses"–Provided by publisher.
Identifiers: LCCN 2023035553 (print) | LCCN 2023035554 (ebook) | ISBN 9798765626443 (library binding) | ISBN 9798765629567 (paperback) | ISBN 9798765636923 (epub)
Subjects: LCSH: Nurses–Juvenile literature. | Nursing–Juvenile literature.
Classification: LCC RT61.5 .L44 2024 (print) | LCC RT61.5 (ebook) | DDC 610.73–dc23/eng/20231207

LC record available at https://lccn.loc.gov/2023035553
LC ebook record available at https://lccn.loc.gov/2023035554

Manufactured in the United States of America
1 - CG - 7/15/24